Leslie

Apple Strudel

Written and Illustrated
by Sarah Burell

A Harcourt Achieve Imprint

www.Rigby.com
1-800-531-5015

Literacy by Design Leveled Readers: *Leslie Ludel's Apple Strudel*

For Leslie Forehand

ISBN-13: 978-1-4189-3905-2
ISBN-10:   1-4189-3905-6

Printed in China
2 3 4 5 6 7 8 985 14 13 12 11 10 09 08

Contents

Chapter 1
The Old Playground..........................5

Chapter 2
Preparing for the Bake Sale.............12

Chapter 3
Leslie, Dad, and Bones......................16

Chapter 4
The Bake Sale......................................26

Chapter 5
**A Playground
to Be Proud Of**....................................36

Chapter 1

The Old Playground

The playground at Olive Pitley Elementary School was falling apart. The concrete was cracked, the monkey bars wobbled, and the merry-go-round was completely out of whack. A metal fence had been put up around the playground, and attached to the fence was a big sign that read, "Danger! Keep Out!"

At recess the kids sat on the school steps and stared miserably at the broken-down equipment.

"It's so depressing," moaned Lucy.

"Someone needs to fix it," said Javier.

"Olive Pitley herself would be embarrassed," said Stacy.

The teachers weren't very happy either. The children needed to be able to run around at recess, and now even the nicest and quietest kids were restless in class. Worse still, Pitley's wildest student, Ferguson Jones, was now a real problem. Ferguson had too much energy—he desperately needed a place to play.

Ms. Lin, Ferguson's teacher, was beside herself. "Settle down, Ferguson! You need to walk!" she cried.

But Ferguson could not keep still.
He bounced off the walls, he bounced
off other kids, and he even bounced into
Ms. Lin and knocked her into old Mr.
Wiggins.

"I need a vacation," said Ms. Lin.

"I need a new broom," sighed
Mr. Wiggins.

Leslie Ludel was as upset about the playground as the other kids, but she didn't just sit around complaining. While Leslie's friends ate lunch and felt sorry for themselves, Leslie was thinking hard of ways to solve the problem of the old playground. "I have to think of something," she said to herself.

After lunch Leslie asked Ms. Lin if she could go and talk to the principal.

She stepped into Mr. Potter's office, a bright room lined with bookcases and important-looking files. On Mr. Potter's desk was a large photograph of his family, as well as several crumpled-up candy bar wrappers—Mr. Potter had a real sweet tooth!

"Hello Ms. Ludel," said Mr. Potter. "What can I do for you?"

Leslie sat in a big chair in front of Mr. Potter's desk.

"I'm here on very important school business," said Leslie.

"Really?" asked the principal. "Well, speak up then!"

"We desperately need to fix our playground," said Leslie.

"I'm sorry," said Mr. Potter, "but the new computer room has already cost the school a lot of money, and we simply don't have any left to improve the playground. In fact, as you can see," he said as he pointed out the window at the fence around the old playground, "we haven't been able to spend money on it for many years."

"We could have a fundraiser," suggested Leslie. "How about a bake sale?"

"What a delicious idea!" said Mr. Potter.

Chapter 2

Preparing for the Bake Sale

The next morning, Mr. Potter made an announcement to the entire school. "Boys and girls," he said. "On Saturday, Olive Pitley Elementary will host a giant bake sale at 12:00 in the cafeteria. Tell your moms, your dads, your aunts, your uncles, your friends, and your neighbors. If we all bring something to sell, we can raise enough money to improve our playground."

"Hooray!" shouted all the kids.

All week everyone at Olive Pitley Elementary talked about the bake sale that was coming up. Each student claimed that he or she would be bringing the very best treats.

"My mom makes the gooiest fudge," bragged Lucy.

"My grandma makes pan dulce from scratch," said Javier.

"My dad bakes extra-extra-extra chocolate brownies," said Stacy.

Ferguson Jones was even more excited than usual. He ran in circles, jumped up and down, and bounced off a few more walls. Ms. Lin tried to stay out of his way.

However, the most excited person by far at Olive Pitley Elementary was Mr. Potter. He dreamed of all the peanut butter cookies, lemon meringue pies, and chocolate cakes he would be buying (and then eating). "I can't wait for Saturday!" he thought.

BAKE SALE

OLIVE PITLEY
ELEMENTARY

SATURDAY
OCTOBER 11, 12:00 PM

Of course, it was Leslie Ludel who suggested that the class make flyers to advertise the sale. They used the new computers to design the flyers and printed enough for all the children in the school to hand out to all of their friends and family.

Then they made some posters and went with their parents to tape them up all over town.

Chapter 3

Leslie, Dad, and Bones

Leslie Ludel lived with her father and her dog, Bones, in a small house on the edge of town. As Leslie walked through the door, Dad greeted her and asked how her day had been. She told him all about her idea for the bake sale.

"I could bake one of my special spicy pepperoni pizzas," said Dad.

"We were thinking that we would sell sweet things, like cookies, cakes, and pies," said Leslie.

"I could try to make a coffee cake," said Dad with a hopeful look on his face.

Leslie knew her father was good at cooking pizzas, but he wasn't very good at baking sweets. "That's OK," said Leslie. "Just keep making your terrific pizzas for us, and when it comes to the bake sale, I'll try to think of *something*."

Bright and early Saturday morning, Leslie turned on her television to watch the *Fun and Fancy Cooking Show.*

"Today," said the chef, "I am going to make a *delightful* apple strudel. It's low in sugar and absolutely perfect for those of us with a sweet tooth!"

Leslie grabbed her notebook.

"First slice up some delicious apples and then cover them with yummy brown sugar. Next add some *delightful* raisins, a sprinkle of cinnamon, and a *lovely* pinch of nutmeg!"

Leslie watched the chef mix the ingredients together and took careful notes.

"Finally," said the chef, "lay out the flaky French pastry, spoon the *glorious* apple mixture into the center, and then fold in the sides of the pastry like this. Then bake in a very hot oven for 15 minutes, and you will have the most *delicious* dessert. *Bon appétit!*"

Bones turned to look at the television and wagged his tail.

Leslie turned off the television and sighed. "Well, it's a good idea, Bones," she said, "but we'll never be able to make that fancy flaky French pastry."

"Why don't you use pizza dough?" asked Dad.

Leslie looked up in surprise. "Dad, I think you've just come up with a great idea!"

Leslie, Dad, and Bones went into the kitchen.

In the refrigerator, Leslie found a tube of ready-made pizza dough. "Who needs fancy flaky pastry?" she muttered. "I can use this dough to make a *delightful* apple strudel, just like the one on the *Fun and Fancy Cooking Show.*"

Leslie searched the kitchen for more ingredients. She found brown sugar in the pantry, a box of raisins in the cupboard, and some small jars of cinnamon and nutmeg on the spice rack.

However, when Dad came back into the kitchen, Leslie was sitting at the table with a frown on her face.

"Dad," she said, "we have a big problem. We don't have any apples!"

"Don't worry, I have an idea," said Dad as he disappeared into the pantry. After a whole lot of banging and clanging, he reappeared holding a can of sliced apples.

"Those will be perfect, and it's so much easier than cutting apples ourselves anyway!" exclaimed Leslie.

Dad turned on the oven while Leslie unrolled the dough onto a cookie sheet. Then Dad opened the can of apples, pouring the slices into a bowl. Using a spoon, Leslie tossed the apples with the brown sugar, raisins, and cinnamon.

Leslie was having fun, and she pretended that she was on television. "And now, ladies and gentlemen," she said, "the most important ingredient—a *lovely* pinch of nutmeg!"

Leslie spooned the mixture onto the dough and folded the dough in place.

"*Bon appetit!*" she said.

Leslie went to the sink to wash her hands, and Dad opened the oven to put the apple strudel inside. But just as Dad was about to place it into the oven, Bones ran into the kitchen. He jumped up at the strudel, knocking it out of Dad's hands.

SPLAT!

"Bones!" cried Leslie. "I said '*Bon appetit*,' not 'Bones gets a treat!'"

Leslie looked at the clock and saw that it was already 11:00! The bake sale would be starting in an hour, and she didn't have time to make anything else.

"OK, Dad, we need to put our heads together," Leslie said. "We need a new plan, and we're running out of time!"

Chapter 4

The Bake Sale

By 12:30, the Olive Pitley Elementary cafeteria was filled with moms, dads, aunts, uncles, friends, and neighbors. Business was booming, and everyone agreed that the bake sale was going well.

Lucy bought cookies for all her friends, and Javier bought a carrot cake for his grandmother. Stacy bought her own

up-side-down cake, because it came out right-side-up, and she was too embarrassed to let anyone see it.

Ferguson Jones came with his mom, who served plates of refreshing fruit salad. Ferguson had his eye on a large chocolate cake. "Don't even think about it, Ferguson," warned his mom. "You'll be bouncing off the walls if you eat that!"

Mr. Potter sat at a table in front of a big chart. He'd never been happier, and the sale was going better than expected.

"Delicious, simply delicious," he said, helping himself to another delicious peanut butter cookie.

His wife, Mrs. Potter, frowned at him and said, "I think you've had quite enough cookies for one day, don't you, dear?"

"But it's for such a good cause!" Mr. Potter said with a grin.

PITLEY BAKE SALE

We can do it !!!

After the first hour, Ms. Lin counted the money and told Mr. Potter how much had been collected.

"Excellent!" exclaimed Mr. Potter. "We're halfway there already!"

He stood up and colored in five gingerbread men on his chart.

An hour later, Ms. Lin counted the money again, and Mr. Potter colored in two more gingerbread men on the chart.

"Not bad," he said.

However, during the last hour of the bake sale, business slowed down.

"I never want to see another cupcake," moaned Lucy.

"I've spent all my money," sighed Javier.

"My dad ate so much and got so full that he fell asleep!" said Stacy. "It's so embarrassing!"

Ms. Lin counted the last of the money, and Mr. Potter colored in one more gingerbread man. No one was buying any more food, and they hadn't quite raised enough money to fix the playground.

Poor Ferguson looked so sad. Not only had the chocolate cake been sold, but it also looked like he wouldn't have anywhere to play at recess after all.

"It's so depressing," moaned Lucy.

"We need a playground," cried Javier.

"It's embarrassing," said Stacy.

After all of the early excitement, a cloud of gloom now descended over the cafeteria.

Just then the cafeteria doors burst open, and in marched Leslie Ludel with her dad. In all the excitement, no one had noticed that Leslie had been missing.

However, Leslie didn't have any cakes or pies or cookies. Instead, she was carrying a large piece of wood.

With the help of her dad, Leslie lifted the wood onto a table. Attached to the wood was an amazing poster.

Leslie had drawn a beautiful apple strudel on the poster, and all around the edges, she had taped handwritten recipe cards.

OLIVE PITLEY
BAKE SALE

Leslie Ludel's Apple Strudel

Recipe $3.

PITLEY

"Your apple strudel looks delicious," said Mr. Potter. "I'd like a recipe card."

"Even I can make this!" said Javier's dad, reading one of the recipe cards.

"It's low in sugar," said Ferguson's mom as she read the ingredients, "so Ferguson can have some of this without bouncing off the walls."

Leslie sold every one of her recipe cards. Ms. Lin added up the money and gave Mr. Potter the final total.

"Fabulous!" cried Mr. Potter as he colored in the last two gingerbread men on the chart. "We've reached our goal, and Olive Pitley Elementary will have a playground to be proud of again."

"Hooray!" shouted the kids.

"Hooray!" shouted the teachers.

"Hooray!" shouted the moms, dads, aunts, uncles, friends, and neighbors.

Chapter 5

A Playground to Be Proud Of

The following week, Mr. Potter announced that there would be a competition to help design the new playground.

Javier wanted a big basketball court with four hoops so lots of kids could play at once.

Stacy had an idea, but she wouldn't show anyone her drawing. "It's too embarrassing!" she cried.

"I have to think of something," sighed Leslie.

In the end, it was Ferguson who came up with the winning design. His idea for a playground was wonderful. There were

things to swing on, things to climb on,
things to crawl under, and plenty of space
left over to run around.

Mr. Potter hired some strong workers to
repair the concrete and build the
new equipment.

The kids loved their new playground.

"It's awesome!" said Lucy.

"I want to play all the time," said Javier.

"It's not embarrassing at all," said
Stacy, "and Olive Pitley herself would be
proud of it."

Ms. Lin watched Ferguson Jones enjoying the new playground. He ran up and down, climbed over things, and crawled under things. And when he came

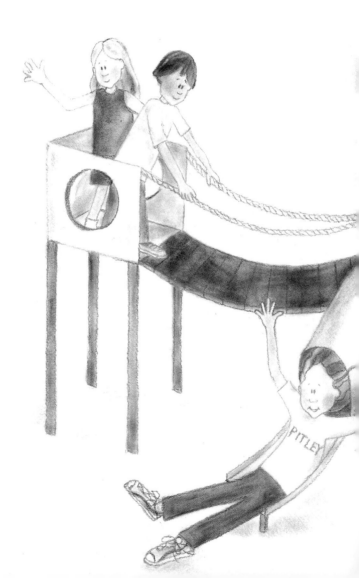

in from recess, he sat down at his desk and got right to work.

"Thank goodness!" said Ms. Lin. "Where would we be without Leslie Ludel and her apple strudel?"

Leslie Ludel's
Apple Strudel Recipe

Ingredients

1 12 oz. tube of pizza crust dough

1 20 oz. can of sliced apples, undrained, or apple pie filling

1 cup brown sugar

1 cup raisins

1 teaspoon cinnamon

A large pinch of nutmeg

What to do

1. Open the pizza crust package and unroll the dough onto a cookie sheet.
2. Mix the apple slices, brown sugar, raisins, and cinnamon in a mixing bowl. Add a large pinch of nutmeg.
3. Spoon the apple mixture onto the pizza dough.
4. Fold up the edges of the pizza dough around the apple mixture. Pinch together the top and both ends.
5. Refrigerate for 30 minutes.
6. With the help of an adult, bake in the oven at 425° Fahrenheit for 15 minutes or until the apple strudel is golden brown.

Bon appetit!